The Wilmington insurrection of 1898:
The Democrats, The Secret Nine, and
The Rise of White Supremacy

By

CHESTER DOUGLAS

TABLE OF CONTENTS

On August 6, 2017, the North Carolina GOP Executive Director, Dallas Woodhouse, used Twitter to go back in time and chastise Democrats for murdering blacks more than a century ago. In response to a tweet from the North Carolina Democratic Party about the Voting Rights Act, Woodhouse tweeted:

"After they murdered blacks in Wilmington @NCDemParty, passed what they called the White Declaration of Independence"

Other Woodhouse tweets included:

"From the party that ran a racist campaign of murder and closed the polls to blacks who were Republicans, gaining power for 100 years"

And...

"The Wilmington Riot of 1898 was not an act of spontaneous violence...The events of Nov. 10, 1898 were a result of the long-range campaign strategy by Democratic Party leaders to regain political control of Wilmington – at that time (the) state's most populous city – and North Carolina in the name of white supremacy"

Why was a Republican leader castigating the Democrats for a race riot from the late-1800s? What was the White Declaration of Independence? What was he even talking about? Although there have been race riots in the United States for centuries that have been researched by historians, scholars, and journalists, in 2017 Woodhouse was referring to a racially violent incident that happened in his own backyard – the Wilmington Insurrection of 1898. And, this was a violent outbreak that, for years, was falsified in history books, educational books, and in conversation. Until recently, this story was lied about for decades. But, this is the true story. And, Woodhouse was correct – the Wilmington Insurrection of 1898 was not a bout of spontaneous violence. Instead, it was a calculated effort by a political party – the Democratic Party – to murder blacks and their white allies, run the rest out of town, and ultimately steal an election.

THE RACIST BACKGROUND
OF THE DEMOCRATS

On November 10, 1898, Conservative Democrats did the unthinkable – they took to the streets as an armed militia, burned down a building that housed an African-American newspaper, murdered blacks and their white allies, and forcefully took over a legally elected government. They did give the African-American newspaper owner warning – end your newspaper and leave town forever, or else. Although the editor did leave town, they still destroyed the newspaper's building, murdered their enemies, and destroyed the landscape of Wilmington, a once racially integrated city.

Led by a former congressman, a white mob caused racially motivated violence that would change a city, a state, and even the racial construction of the United States. This group of whites even used what they called a "White Declaration of Independence" to further support their inflammatory rhetoric in support of white supremacy. The result was the banishment of African Americans from the city, their white counterparts, the Republicans and Populists who were elected to run the city, and anyone else who was in the Conservative Democrats' way. They even put together a militia called the Red Shirts to further the violence and intimidation. Finally, the Democrats cheated in the North Carolina elections two days before their violent attack to further steal the local and state governments.

Some have called this horrible blemish in North Carolina's vast history a race riot, others have called it a revolution, and still others have used probably one of the most appropriate terms – a coup d'etat. This violent event from North Carolina's past has also been deemed the Wilmington Insurrection of 1898, the Wilmington Massacre of 1898, and the Wilmington Race Riot of 1898. No matter the term, this racist time was the most dangerous, racially violent event in North Carolina's history and a turning point in North Carolina politics. Up until recently, however, these tumultuous times remained hidden from North Carolina's vast history. Why?

Those who have written about the events that happened in Wilmington in 1898 were not always accurate – for years the Wilmington Insurrection of 1898 was thought to be a race riot caused by blacks. Even worse, the white Conservative Democrats were deemed as heroes, not murderers. It took nearly a century for the true story of this racist, violent time in Wilmington to finally surface -- a group of hateful, white supremacists destroyed a black newspaper, killed innocent black and white victims, and overthrew a duly-elected government in what is seen today as the only coup d'etat to ever happen on American soil.

A CALCULATED PLAN
OF WHITE SUPREMACY

The events that took over Wilmington in 1898 did not happen overnight and they were not the result of spontaneous violence; instead, they were the result of a premeditated and deliberate campaign by some of the area's most prominent Democrats who campaigned on one issue: white supremacy. These leading figures in North Carolina's political history would not only succeed in constructing a one-party state built on hate and racism. Their actions would also be just the beginning of the rise of white supremacy and "Jim Crow" throughout the United States. And what was even more disturbing, the actions taken on that fateful day were a highly-calculated plan by a group of racist, white Democrats. Their plan had four distinctive parts:

1. Steal the local and state elections away from Republicans and Populists –The Democratic Party decided to first run on one issue: white supremacy. When that did not work to lure voters away from the other two parties – Republicans and Populists – they used threats to blacks and Republican and Populist whites so they would not vote; intimidation from a group of armed militants called the "Red Shirts"; disseminated hateful, racist anti-black propaganda through pamphlets and in the media; and even stuffed ballot boxes with Democratic votes in order to steal the statewide elections on November 8, 1868.

2. Start a riot – Two days after they stole the elections, on November 10, 1868, white men attacked a building that

housed an African American-owned newspaper in Wilmington, burned it to the ground, and then went on to attack, torture, and kill blacks and their white allies throughout the city.

3. Stage a coup d'etat – While the riotous violence was evolving throughout the city, a band of white Democrats, led by a former congressman, would then use their armed militia of Red Shirts to force the Republican and Populist white leaders who were not up for re-election on November 8 – the mayor of Wilmington, the chief of police, and other local leaders – to resign from office. The Democrats were ultimately in charge of the city.

4. Forcibly remove the opposition – Once the Republicans and Populists were out of office, the Democrats then made sure they stayed out of office by taking them, by gunpoint, to the train station and banishing them from the city. Both black and white individuals of power were forced to leave the city they had once called home, a city that was once a symbol of black hope.

There will be many names read throughout this book who contributed to the violence on that fateful day in 1898. Some names that are notable include: Furnifold Simmons, who led the Democratic Party's 1898 campaign and was the mastermind behind the violent attacks; Alfred M. Waddell, the mouthpiece and leader of the attacks themselves; and Charles B. Aycock, who used the power of public speaking (along with Waddell) to enrage white voters to turn on their black neighbors along with the whites who protected them. Yet, these three men were not the only Conservative Democratic leaders to stage the coup and the violent attacks. Hundreds upon hundreds of white men followed their lead.

In fact, on November 10, 1898, a mob of more than 1,500 heavily armed white men attacked a building that housed an African American-owned newspaper called the *Wilmington Daily Record* in Wilmington, North Carolina. In the name of what the men believed was white supremacy, they burned the newspaper's building to the ground and left the African-American men who worked there, and lived throughout Wilmington, to either flee or be killed – countless black residents were killed on that fateful day. This racist white mob then seized control of the rightfully elected Republican government in a coup d'etat that would go down in history and contribute to white supremacy and the racist segregation known as "Jim Crow." This story was hidden for decades until the Wilmington Race Riot Commission was established in 2000 to develop an accurate historical record of the event and even recommend payments to the descendants of the victims. By 2006, the real story of what happened on November 10, 1898 was finally told. But, what exactly led up to this attack? This racism did not happen overnight; it stemmed from slavery, freedom, and white supremacy.

HOW DID WILMINGTON
GET TO THAT FATEFUL DAY?

In order to understand the Wilmington Insurrection of 1898, one must first understand North Carolina's role in the Civil War. Except for Tennessee, North Carolina had waited longer than any other state to split from the Union and join the Confederacy during the Civil War. This was not because North Carolinians were against slavery; on the contrary, North Carolina residents staunchly supported the institution of slavery. North Carolinians, however, saw secession as a serious choice away from the Constitutional protections of the Union. That being said, the North and the South disagreed on many things – from slavery and trade to tariffs and individual state rights – and on May 20, 1861, North Carolina seceded from the Union and officially entered the Civil War.

Over the next four years, America would be embroiled in a Civil War that took the lives of between 640,000 and 700,000 soldiers until the surrendering of General Robert E. Lee on April 9, 1865. One must remember why the Civil War was fought – it was fought over the moral issue of slavery. Although the North and South disagreed on other issues, it was the economics of slavery and the politics behind it that led to what some historians say ended up being the bloodiest conflict in America's history. North Carolina alone lost more than 30,000 soldiers from battle and disease. Ultimately, the Union won the battle and North Carolina underwent a time of Reconstruction enforced by the North.

After the assassination of President Abraham Lincoln, his predecessor, President Andrew Johnson, tried to continue Lincoln's endeavors of reconcile between the Confederate South and the Union in the North. The government developed a constitutional amendment to abolish slavery, and unite the young country. The Thirteenth Amendment of the United States Constitution was ratified by the states on December 6, 1865, and was the first amendment to even mention the institution of slavery. Not only did the Thirteenth Amendment abolish slavery and involuntary servitude, it also granted Congress the power to enact laws to enforce the amendment. These actions were a turning point in America, as they finally gave blacks freedom.

North Carolina saw similar endeavors; under military rule after the war, a proclamation deemed all southerners, except individuals in leadership or the very rich, pardoned in the Southern states as long as they swore an oath of loyalty to their country and the United States Constitution. A second proclamation appointed a provisional governor of North Carolina, former Whig and Democrat turned Republican, William W. Holden. Appointed directly by President Johnson in 1865, Holden was then officially elected governor of North Carolina in 1868 and served through 1871. Holden was ultimately impeached – only the second governor in American history and the first to be removed from office – after the Democrats regained majorities in both houses of the state legislatures.

Under Republican rule, North Carolina ratified the Fourteenth Amendment in 1868, which officially resulted in the state's recognition of Reconstruction. The Fourteenth Amendment addressed numerous aspects of citizenship, giving equal protection of the laws. When this amendment was ratified on July 28, 1868, it also was one of the "Reconstruction amendments" added to the Constitution to guarantee rights and privileges to former slaves. Democrats, however, resented what they saw as an abrupt and radical change in their state.

The newly emancipated slaves, called "freedmen," were enthusiastic to finally be able to vote, and then were greatly inclined to vote for the Republican Party. This was not a surprise, as it was the Republicans, led by Republican President Abraham Lincoln, who had emancipated blacks and gave them their freedoms under the Fourteenth Amendment even after his assassination. After Lincoln's untimely death, the Republican Party was still viewed as the party of Lincoln, his ideals, and emancipation. These new freedoms, coupled with a temporary period in which Confederate veterans were banned from holding office or even voting, estranged the white Democrats even more during this time of Reconstruction.

LIFE AFTER THE CIVIL WAR

After the Civil War, North Carolina was just one of many states that felt the economic impact of the war. In addition, the state itself now had two very different and distinct political parties – the Republican Party, which favored and was supported by blacks, and the Democratic Party, which was supported more by rural, working class whites. Although the Democratic Party did have political control in the state from 1876 through 1894, this control unraveled as the state moved closer and closer to an economic depression.

The Republican Party, on the other hand, gained power in North Carolina, mainly because of the support the party received from blacks who now were given the power to vote through the Fourteenth Amendment. These and other events spurred early bouts of violence – rebellious veterans joined the Ku Klux Klan to help arrange violent events at elections with the hopes of suppressing the black vote. In fact, there were some state legislatures in the North and the South that were actually controlled by members of the Ku Klux Klan.

The Ku Klux Klan was a powerful force in the 1800s – although the group was founded in 1865 in Tennessee, in only five years it would have groups in nearly every southern state. This racist group became a primary vehicle against the Republican Party's Reconstruction-era policies that aspired to establish both political and economic equality for African Americans after the Civil War. African-American participation in public life was one of the biggest changes from Reconstruction, with black leaders now participating, and winning, local, statewide, and even federal elections. The

Ku Klux Klan knew that the groups focus needed to fight this by dedicating its resources to promoting violence against both Republican leaders and Republican voters. And, color did not matter during this underground campaign. If you were a Republican, the Ku Klux Klan would violently protest you no matter if you were white or black.

The Ku Klux Klan became a violent eyesore for Republicans; the group waged an underground campaign that specifically targeted both white and black Republican leaders. The organization had one primary goal – to re-establish white supremacy into America's political realm. And they knew there was one main way to do this, and that was to help support Democratic victories in state legislatures across the South.

In North Carolina, these racist, white supremacist outlets were used to the advantage of the Conservative Democrats. And, they worked -- Democrats would end up regaining control of the state legislature through the oration of political powerhouses and a new vigilant group, the "Red Shirts," that would form in North Carolina to continue the racist and violent acts of some white Democrats. Although throughout history, the white sheets of the Ku Klux Klan have become a well-known symbol of racism, hate, and murder, the Red Shirts, donned in shirts that were the color of their group's name, also symbolized violence and hate. In the minds of black people living in 1898, the Red Shirts were a symbol of fear – they were men who were actually enthusiastic about committing violent acts against blacks and their white supporters.

Even with the help of the Red Shirts, success for the Democrats leading up to the 1898 election did not happen overnight – the Democrats first needed stop a fusion that would take over the local and state government by two political parties: the Republicans and the Populists. Although Republicans were following the word of Lincoln, Confederates and Whigs were banning together to form a Conservative Party that viewed Congress's Reconstruction policies as too radical for states. Then, in 1894, Republicans and Populists, led by a North Carolinian named Leonidas LaFayette Polk, came to an agreement to combine forces against those Conservative Democrats. The Populists were comprised of white rebels protesting against economic issues they saw in their state. Calling themselves the "People's Party," they also saw the opportunity to build an alliance with blacks who shared their values on the economy and then join forces with Republicans, who had long supported black freedom. This "Fusion" coalition was highly successful by campaigning on a variety of popular issues for both whites and blacks. By championing everything from free education to the black man's right to vote, this Fusion movement won every statewide office in both 1894 and 1896.

A NEW FORM
OF POLITICS: FUSION

In order to understand North Carolina's political system, one must understand the three parties that dominated North Carolina politics in the 1800s. The Democratic Party supported slave holding, developed into a firm alliance of wealthy, working class whites, and dominated the North Carolina state and local governments through 1894. The Republicans, on the other hand, were the anti-slavery party that campaigned on racial tolerance, free enterprise, and political equality for whites and blacks. Yet, there was one more party in North Carolina – the Populist Party. Known as the "People's Party" the Populist Partywas founded by working class whites, mostly farmers, who left the Democratic Party.

In the late-1800s, an economic depression increased in North Carolina, which spurred an alliance between the Republicans and the Populists known as the "Fusion Movement." The Republicans and the Populists catered to very different voters, and by fusing these voters together they hoped to defeat the reign of the Democrats. This new brand of Fusionists were very different from the Democrats – they campaigned for a local self-government, free public education, electoral reforms, and, most importantly, voting rights for black men. All in all, the Fusionists allowed for more African-American involvement and participation in the government.

The white Conservative Democrats were faced with constant defeat during this time; new Reconstruction-era laws were disturbing to the political group, the state Supreme Court was constantly ruling against them, and the Fusion between the Republicans and the Populists continued to gain more power and support. For example, the Fusionists focused on popular economic issues North Carolinians were facing, such as debt relief desperately needed by both races after the Civil War. Focusing on economic depression was a smart move for the Fusionists, as economic grievances were shared by both blacks and whites throughout the state. In addition, they were focusing on their base – newly free blacks and working-class whites. Through their interracial "Fusion" alliance, the Populists and the Republicans advocated for these two groups and the freedoms of both races.

These fused candidates defeated Democratic candidates in statewide elections and the fused party won legislature majority in the mid-1860s. In addition, this fused government also enacted a concept called "home rule," which mean local officials in North Carolina would be elected by the people, not appointed by the state. This meant they began transferring those appointed Democratic positions to popularly elected positions, and those elected by the populous were the Fusionists. Remember, their alliance had the ever-popular and growing black vote throughout North Carolina along with the working-class whites. The Fusionists knew they had the popular vote on their side.

The Fusionists' political dominance was clear, as they won elections in every statewide office in both 1894 and 1896. The party even won the highest appointment of the state – Republican politician Daniel L. Russell was elected governor. Although Russell was once a prominent slave owner, he later became a leader in the Republican Party (which also made him a target of the Conservative press, particularly the *News and Observer,* which played a main role in the Wilmington Insurrection of 1898). Weighing in at nearly 300 pounds, Governor Russell pledged his support to black advancement and appealed to black voters. With these pledges, home rule, and the fusion between Republicans and Populists and their encouragement of the black vote, the fused party retained control of the legislature until the Conservative Democrats would ultimately steal the elections in 1898.

In Wilmington, the Fusion victory gave political power to both races – whites and blacks – by allowing voters to pick their own candidates (home rule) and encouraging the rights of all. Now, as with any fused relationship, the Republicans and Populists did have their issues of disagreement. In addition, some white Fusionists were not as supportive of racial equality as their counterparts would have hoped in the post-Civil War era. In fact, at one point the Populists offered to fuse with the Democratic Party – both parties were majorly controlled by whites – but the Democrats refused their offer. Although the Populists originally only had the support from a tiny number of blacks holding public offices, the Democrats and, more specifically, wealthy white men, fought on their own and swore that they would regain control of the North Carolina government. The Democrats had a powerful, yet quiet, group of supporters: the white supremacists. And, in the minds of the white supremacists, black votes could sway the elections towards the Fusionists, and this sway in votes had to be stopped.

But, how would the Democrats regain control of a government that had a very large, new voting base in free African-American voters? Simply put, they would remove blacks from the political equation. This is because the number of blacks in Wilmington rivaled many other cities. In fact, the numbers spoke for themselves. As North Carolina's largest city, two-thirds of the population was comprised of African Americans in the 1890s. Wilmington's African-American community participated in politics more than African Americans in other North Carolina towns, and these African Americans more than likely would vote against the Conservative Democrats.

THE CONSERVATIVE DEMOCRATS' ULTIMATE PLAN

First, the Democrats fostered a plan to reverse the "home rule" election process instituted by the Fusionists. This action would allow them to slowly gain political control first through the judiciary and then later through a divisive political campaign to put whites against blacks. Not all whites were accepting of black freedom, and with the rise of blacks in the state came a rise in racial tensions. The Democrats saw this and used it to their advantage. In 1897, Democrats started to realize that they would need to focus, not on blacks or white supporters of blacks, but resentful whites who were looking for change from Reconstruction-era politics. The Democrats decided they need an issue – one single issue – that would all but destroy the alliance between whites and blacks living across the state.

By 1898, the fateful year of Wilmington's violent, racist destruction, the city's political power was in the hands of four Fusionist leaders. There was the white Republican mayor, Dr. Silas P. Wright; white Fusionist and acting sheriff and political confidant to Governor Russell, George Zadoc French; Republican Postmaster W. H. Chadbourn, who was originally from the North; and respected businessman and Wilmington property owner, Flaviel W. Foster. Foster in particular had a considerable amount of support from black voters. Foster was not a southern, Confederate man; instead, he was a Pennsylvania native and had served in the Union Army during the Civil War. He was also close friends with Governor Russell and even named his son after him – Daniel Russell Foster. These four men were commonly known as "The Ring."

The Ring had a large amount of control over the Republican Party, consisting of approximately 2,000 black voters and more than 100 whites, along with approximately twenty wealthy and affluent Wilmington businessmen. The Ring also used the media to disseminate its political power, most notably *Wilmington Post* and the African-American-owned newspaper, *The Wilmington Daily Record.*

In the years that followed Reconstruction and under Republican and Fusionist rule, blacks aspired to finally be out of slavery and make lives for themselves – lives of prosperity and freedom. Blacks aspired to be everything from businessmen to farmers, and the city of Wilmington in particular gave them these opportunities under The Ring and other leaders. Wilmington was a leading example of black hope and prosperity in this new world of freedom in post-Civil War America. The city also had a strong religious community that supported charitable organizations and education for African Americans, and African Americans were found to contribute successfully to the economy. They were even managing their own businesses and buying homes throughout Wilmington.

These were educated, professional black individuals – the black male literacy rate in Wilmington was actually higher than white males – and these black men were contributing to a growing middle class society in the state's largest city. For example, a black entrepreneur named Thomas Miller was one of Wilmington's three real estate agents, while another man, Frederick Sadgwar, was an African-American architect. Whether they worked in real estate, architecture, finance, or politics, many African Americans held very prominent leadership roles in the city. African Americans also held careers in everything from plumbing, to mechanics, to tailoring, to even watchmaking. In addition, many former slaves put their skills to use, whether it was in baking, dyeing, or other service positions. Wilmington was truly a symbol of black achievement after a war that raged for civil rights for all – North and South, black and white.

African Americans also leaned towards the Republican and Fusionist Parties, which were biracial. In Wilmington, black individuals held local offices and were continuing to attain prominent positions within the city. But as African Americans continued to advance politically, economically, and even socially, racial tensions between whites and blacks also grew. For example, there was now competition between uneducated whites who were competing with blacks in the job market. There were also wealthy whites who thought they were unfairly paying higher property taxes than their black counterparts.

Political strife, the Thirteenth and Fourteenth Amendments, freedom for both former slaves and women in general – the era immediately following the Civil War and emancipation, the Reconstruction Era, was a turning point in American history. There were many, many achievements during this era, yet this fight for freedom for all led to a violent outcome: white supremacist backlash. And, the turning point in the post-Reconstruction world of North Carolina politics was the Wilmington Insurrection of 1898.

LEADING TOWARDS
THE 1898 VIOLENCE

T he violence that hit Wilmington in 1898 was a representation of racist, white supremacist ideals that many whites still held throughout the South. It was a message from white supremacists against the protections under the Thirteenth and Fourteenth Amendments and a reminder to those in support of these freedoms that "whiteness" would overshadow the newly created rights of blacks. One man who began the rise of white supremacy in North Carolina was Furnifold Simmons.

Furnifold Simmons was born in Jones County, North Carolina in 1854. He was a graduate of Trinity University (now Duke University) and studied law. Politics would be his calling, however, and Simmons served one term in Congress between 1887 and 1889 before losing the next two elections. Yet, his knack for politics would be essential in 1898 when he would be in charge of forming a band of white men to restore the party's power. In 1900, the legislature appointed him a seat in the United States Senate, which he held for 30 years. Simmons was also chairman of the Finance Committee for six years and, unsuccessfully, ran for president of the United States in 1920. In 1898, however, he was simply in charge of spreading the issue of white supremacy for the Conservative Democrats.

Simmons became well known in the Democratic Party after running a successful campaign in 1892 and was appointed party chairman of the 1898 campaign. Simmons knew that winning political offices in 1898 would not be easy; therefore, he decided that his party would not focus on various economic, political, and social issues like the Fusionists. Instead, the

Democrats would focus on one, single issue: white supremacy. He figured this would be the one issue that would cross party lines, the one issue that would exacerbate the racial resentment that was still felt across the South.

There was a reason Simmons was the perfect choice for the job as Democratic Party Chairman: he had powerful connections with white men who shared his Democrats racist views. These men would ultimately help him strategize a comeback for the Democratic Party. He chose his first group of leaders carefully:

Charles Brantley Aycock – Born in 1859, Aycock was the youngest of ten children and a graduate from the University of North Carolina. He practiced law in Goldsboro and then became a former lawyer turned Democratic Party leader who defended white supremacy. He was also an advocate for public education, yet strongly endorsed segregated schooling due to his white supremacy values. In 1900, he defended the mob violence he was a part of starting in 1898 by saying it was to preserve the peace. Aycock would end up serving as the 50th governor of North Carolina from 1901 through 1905 and supported a school tax plan based on color: white taxes would fund white public schools and black taxes would fund black public schools. In 1912, he ran for United States Senate against his friend, Furnifold Simmons, but did not live to see the result. His life ended with some irony; he died on April 4, 1912 while he was delivering a speech on education.

Henry G. Conner – Wilmington-born Conner attained his license to practice law at only nineteen years old and would later be appointed to the Senate of 1885 chairman of the Judiciary Committee. As a staunch Democrat, Conner was nominated in 1894 to the North Carolina Supreme Court by none other than the Populist Party. Although he criticized the

Democrats' appeal of racial prejudice, he was still an active participant in the 1898 Democratic white supremacy campaign.

Robert Brodnax Glenn – Glenn was also a North Carolina native who, before helping lead the Wilmington Insurrection of 1898, was a prosecuting attorney in his home state, served as United States Attorney for the Western District of North Carolina, and was even elected to the North Carolina Senate the same year he led the racial violence. He later became governor of North Carolina in 1904.

Claude Kitchin – Kitchin was appointed to the North Carolina Democratic Executive Committee and helped mobilize the most destructive group for the Democrats: the "Red Shirts." He also played a major role in what was called "trick ballot boxes" that only counted certain votes, which is how he was elected as congressman of his own district. In addition, racism ran in his family. His brother, Congressman William Walton Kitchin, was quoted as saying, "Before we allow the Negroes to control this state as they do now…we will kill enough of them that there will not be enough left to bury them." W. W. Kitchin would serve numerous terms in Congress before being elected as Governor of North Carolina. Like his brother, Claude was on the House Ways and Means Committee and became House Majority Leader, illustrating the power of the Kitchin brothers.

Locke Craig – A statehouse member for two terms and a friend of Aycock's since their childhood, Craig took a leading role in the group's white supremacy campaign both on the ground and in the House.

Cameron Morrison – Active in politics since he was a child, Morrison had an impressive political employment history. Although he started his political career as a Republican, he quickly switched to the Democrats and won the recognition of his peers for leading the deadly "Red Shirt" movement into violent outbreaks against Republican and Fusionist candidates and black voters. He would end up serving as mayor of Rockingham and the state senate before attaining the highest recognition – governor of North Carolina – from 1921 through 1925.

George Rountree – Rountree was an attorney and judge before entering the Republican Party and its white supremacy campaigns. He was elected to the General Assembly under the Republicans' reign and served as chairman of the committee on constitutional reform, which drafted the Grandfather Clause – males could only vote if they could read and write or if their grandfather voted, which would automatically eliminate black men.

Francis Donnell Winston – A lawyer with an interest in politics, Winston was one of North Carolina's leading Democrats and was elected to the state senate. He also had a major hand in the white supremacy movement – Winston helped organize and promote the creation of white supremacy clubs, which he disguised under the name "White government unions." When his friend, Charles B. Aycock, became governor, Winston would accept an appointment as a judge of the Superior Court for the Second Judicial District before himself being elected as lieutenant governor under fellow white supremacist fighter, Governor Robert Brodnax Glenn.

Josephus Daniels – Unlike many of his counterparts, Daniels was not born in North Carolina but, instead, was born in the North, in Washington, D.C. in 1862. His mother moved to Wilson, North Carolina after his father was killed before Daniels even turned three years old. Daniels originally entered the newspaper field with his brother, Charles, when he was only sixteen years old, and he addressed different political issues through the *Cornucopia, Our Free Blade* and the *Free Press.* He studied law at the University of North Carolina and was admitted to the bar in 1885, although never actually practiced law. Instead, he continued his reign in the media with a few small acquisitions before purchasing the popular (and

Conservative) *News and Observer* out of Raleigh, North Carolina. This was his tie to the white supremacy campaign – Daniels used the *News and Observer* to promote the Democratic Party, its white supremacy positions, and Jim Crow laws. In fact, the *News and Observer* ended up becoming a key instrument in the white supremacy campaign. Editorials in his newspaper sensationalized crimes committed by blacks while at the same time reinforcing white supremacist views. His newspaper became so popular that media mogul William Randolph Hearst offered Daniels $1 million for it – Daniels refused. Later in life, Daniels would be named secretary of the Navy by President Woodrow Wilson in 1913 during World War I and then appointed ambassador to Mexico by President Franklin D. Roosevelt in 1933 through 1941. Daniels died on January 15, 1948.

As noted by the impressive resumes above, Simmons surrounded himself with leaders whose names ended up being immortalized on school buildings and street signs throughout North Carolina. These men held the highest political offices in North Carolina throughout the late 1800s and early 1900s. And, this group of men had one thing in common: they all believed the Democrats should have a common theme to help whites and, more specifically, poor whites, so that they were emancipated from what the group called "Negro domination." Now, it should be noted that African-American men did not dominate North Carolina's political system – this "Negro domination" was false. This fact was reiterated by a scholar from North Carolina Central University, Helen G. Edmonds: "An examination of 'Negro domination' in North Carolina revealed that one Negro was elected to Congress; ten to the state legislature; four aldermen were elected in Wilmington, two in New Bern, two in Greenville, one or two in Raleigh, one county treasurer and one county coroner in New Hanover; one register of deeds in Craven; one Negro jailer in Wilmington; and one county commissioner in Warren and one in Craven." As Edmonds noted, this

Negro domination was misleading – the numbers spoke for themselves. Reality and facts were not the basis of the Democratic Party, however. While the Republicans and Fusionists focused on numerous economic, political, and social issues, "Negro domination" would be the racist theme of the 1898 Democratic campaign. This racist theme was then connected to one issue and one issue only: white supremacy.

On November 20, 1897, the Democratic Executive Committee met in Raleigh, North Carolina, to discuss their statewide campaign. Immediately following this meeting, a statewide call for what they said was white unity was issued by Francis D. Winston of Bertie County. Winston was a North Carolina politician and judge who would end up serving as Lieutenant Governor of North Carolina under Governor Robert B. Glenn from 1905 through 1909. But in 1897, he was a mouthpiece for a published call for whites to rise up against blacks. He painted a clear picture of the Republican-Populist fusion as evil and even apocalyptic, and that only the Democrats could save whites from this tyranny. He attacked Republican and Populist leaders and constructed a narrative of hope, hope only obtainable from the Democrats. It was not surprising, then, that Daniel Schenck, a Democratic Party leader, would say about the 1898 election that, "It will be the meanest, vilest, dirtiest campaign since 1876. The slogan of the Democratic Party from the mountains to the sea will be but one word...Nigger." Schenck actually said the 1898 election would be dirtier than the election that ended reconstruction in the South.

As the November 1898 election emerged, the fused party of Populists and Republicans anticipated more success through this "Fusion." They were not prepared for the Democrats and their band of white men who would take their message of white supremacy across the state, however.

23

THE DEMOCRATIC
PLAN IN ACTION

immons had already developed a strong Democratic Party system that would use a combination of printed media sympathetic to white supremacy, propaganda, and speechmaking throughout the state. Simmons basically summarized his vision of the Democratic Party's platform when he stated: "The battle has been fought, the victory is within our reach. North Carolina is a WHITE MAN'S State, and WHITE MEN will rule it, and they will crush the party of negro domination beneath a majority so overwhelming that no other party will ever again dare to attempt to establish negro rule here. They CANNOT intimidate us; they CANNOT buy us, and they SHALL NOT cheat us out of the fruits of our victory." Again and again, Simmons and his followers continued to promote the illusion of Negro domination to scare whites and alienate blacks.

Along with Simmons, Charles Aycock also started the promotion of this white supremacy machine in May when he presented his speech at the Democratic State Convention. Fellow white supremacy advocate Josephus Daniels was housed in Raleigh and spearheaded anti-black propaganda through his media outlets and connections. This propaganda would be at the forefront of Simmons' plan. At this point, Daniels was both the editor and publisher of his Conservative news outlet, the *News and Observer,* and used this power of the pen to disseminate white supremacist propaganda to its readers.

The Conservative newspaper portrayed black men as oversexualized beasts who preyed on white women and used illustrations to promote fear of a "Negro Rule." Through the media, Democrats played on the worst fear for white males – which their precious white women were in danger from oversexualized black males. Daniels had a twenty-one-year-old cartoonist named Norman Jennett who was acclimated to working at a newspaper that promoted white supremacy. For example, on September 27, 1898, the *News and Observer,* printed a cartoon that Jennett penned entitled "The Vampire that Hovers Over North Carolina (Negro Rule)." This racist cartoon portrayed an African-American man as a satanic vampire who dominated and terrorized white men and women. According to Jennett, "the dominant theme of the image is the idea that African-American political power poses a grave danger to white society." Norman Jennett was gifted $63 by Democrats for his work and would end up working for the *New York Journal* and *The Evening Telegram.* Before those successes, however, his racist cartoon was just one of many that featured anti-black rhetoric that would spread across North Carolina leading up to the violence in Wilmington.

Daniels was also seen as a master of sensational headlines, from simple ones like "Negro Control in Wilmington" to more outlandish ones like "A Negro Insulted the Postmistress Because He Did Not Get A Letter" or even "Negro On A Train With Big Feet Behind White." While Daniels was building his propaganda campaign out of Raleigh, another newspaper called the *Charlotte Daily Observer,* based in Charlotte, North Carolina also represented the conservative and racist sentiments of the Democratic Party. The newspaper ran headlines like "The Anglo Saxon/A Great White Man's Rally," while H.E.C. "Red Buck" Bryant, a reporter for the newspaper, traveled throughout North Carolina reporting anti-black, and anti-Fusion, articles in his newspaper.

At one point, the *Charlotte Daily Observer* even rejoiced in the overwhelming success of the bigoted Conservative campaign, bragging about how "The business men of the State are largely responsible for the victory. Not before in years have the bank men, the mill men, and the business men in general — the back-bone of the property interest of the State — taken such sincere interest. They worked from start to finish, and furthermore they spent large bits of money in behalf of the cause." This "cause," as noted in the *Charlotte Daily Observer,* was spreading white supremacy views through violence, intimidation, and taking over the local and state government by force. This "cause" was through the banishing of black and white men who did not fall in line with white supremacy and the Conservative Democrats. This was the "cause" that Simmons and his followers would use the media to propagate and celebrate as blacks and white Fusionists who stood in their way would either be exiled or killed.

Simmons continued to recruit media outlets in North Carolina that he would find were sympathetic to white supremacy: *The Caucasian* and *The Progressive Farmer,* for example, portrayed blacks as disrespectful to whites, branded them as corrupt, and made the claims that black men had an interest in white women that was equating to their continuous theme of "Negro domination." In addition, he disseminated small handbills throughout the streets of Wilmington to further intimidate blacks from voting and white Republicans from speaking out. The flyers read: "These degenerate sons of the white race who control the republican machine in this county, or those whose positions made them influential in putting negro rule on the whites, will suffer the penalty of their responsibility for any disturbance consequent on the determination of the white men of this county to carry the election at any cost."

Although the handbill did not come right out and list the six white offenders, the *Wilmington Messenger* had no problem calling the men out directly, including four members of "The Ring" discussed earlier: Wilmington Mayor Silas Wright, Deputy Sheriff George Z. French, businessmen William H. Chadbourn, and Flavel W. Foster. The pamphlet also called out two additional white men: Police Chief John Melton and lawyer Caleb B. Lockey. Melton in particular would end up receiving numerous letters, all anonymous, that contained the handbills. He and the others feared for their lives against the Democrats and their reign of white supremacists. Melton and the other five white men knew they were on bided time when it came to their careers and even their lives in Wilmington.

Making things worse for the Fusionists was the fact that, unlike the Democrats, they did not have the media on their side. In 1897, North Carolina State Senator Marion Butler, who was a leader of the North Carolina Populist Party, wrote about his own acknowledgement of how important the media would be in 1868: "There is but one chance and but one hope for the railroads to capture the next legislature, and that is for the 'nigger' to be made the issue" with the Raleigh and Charlotte papers "together in the same bed shouting 'nigger.'" Butler's words would hold true, as this was exactly how the Democrats would take the 1898 political elections.

After Simmons constructed the Democratic campaign around white supremacy using his friends and the media, he partnered with nine more prominent men from Wilmington who were against fusion government and blacks in general. These men all had two things in common: they were prominent and influential within the city of Wilmington, and they were all angry with what they called "Negro Rule." These two characteristics made them the perfect team for Simmons to put together a powerful coup that would end up taking over North Carolina's government by force. It would be these nine men who would have a hand in organizing an armed militia to take over the city streets and even identify who should be exiled from Wilmington or even killed – that is, which black and white Fusionists were too dangerous to their plan.

The men – Hardy L. Fennell, William Gilchrist, W. A. Johnson, E. S. Lathrop, P. B. Manning, Hugh MacRae, Walter L. Parsley, L. B. Sasser, and J. Allen Taylor – had already conspired successfully to take control of the government. Simmons' partnership with them brought money and connections to help spread his goal of white supremacy. They would be known as "The Secret Nine." As Democratic editor, Thomas W. Clawson, wrote in his newspaper, the *Wilmington Messenger,* when looking back on this time years later, "for a period of six to 12 months prior to November 10, [1898], the white citizens of Wilmington prepared quietly but effectively for the day when action would be necessary." The Secret Nine were exactly who Clawson would be referring to, a group of nine very influential citizens who instigated a coup behind the scenes for the Democrats. For example, Walter L. Parsley was the owner of Hilton Lumber Company and was a well-known community leader. In 1913, he would donate over two acres of land to New Hanover County for school use and, in turn, an elementary school was named after him. An elementary school was named after one of the Secret Nine, not uncommon for many of the white supremacy men discussed throughout this book. The Secret Nine also appointed George Rountree in the state legislature in order to have an assurance that blacks would be kept from voting. Rountree made sure white Republicans were not able to align with blacks again on a political level. How was this done? Fellow confidant Francis Winston introduced a suffrage bill to keep blacks from voting on January 6, 1899. Rountree would end up chairing the special joint committee that oversaw this amendment, giving them the ultimate power to circumvent the United States Constitution, which had actually given blacks the right to vote.

North Carolina Democrats continually declared that political office should only be held by white men and accused their fused and Republican opponents of reinforcing what they called a "negro domination." At this time, many African-American men did hold positions of power in North Carolina's government, and the Democrats used this to their advantage in their campaigning against Republicans. Calling themselves the white man's party, the Democrats appealed to white North Carolina residents by creating propaganda, holding powerful public speaking events, and intimidating those against them. Simmons' campaign was successful by focusing on one single event: white supremacy. And, what better way to get this event into the forefront than to use the media, that is the media outlets that were sympathetic and, in some respects, even supportive of white supremacy.

Simmons made sure he used his funds wisely in building his white supremacist campaign. He made secret alliances with banks and railroads, promising that Democrats would cut taxes in exchange for monetary donations. Probably the most successful arm of their statewide racist campaign, however, was the speeches made across the state. Simmons was surrounded by some of the best orators who also shared his racist views of white supremacy.

THE POWER OF PUBLIC SPEAKING AND
ALFRED MOORE WADDELL

One of the orators who would also play an integral role in the Wilmington Insurrection of 1898 was former four-time Congressman and Democratic candidate for mayor, Alfred Moore Waddell. Waddell had an impressive family pedigree – he was the great-grandson of Colonel Hugh Waddell, Brigadier General Francis Nash, and of a U.S. Supreme Court Justice who carried his namesake, Alfred Moore. Waddell was an early supporter of the American Party before the Civil War, but joined the Confederacy in 1861 once the war erupted. He fought as a lieutenant colonel for the Confederacy before turning to law, the media, and finally politics. He ended up resigning in August 1864 and returned to Wilmington to start a law firm with his father, Hugh Waddell.

Waddell also had an impressive stint in politics, serving four times in Congress on the Conservative Democratic ticket in 1870, 1872, 1874, and 1876. Waddell would be defeated by Republican Daniel L. Russell in 1878, however. Although his political career was over, Waddell was still active in the Democratic Party along with other groups throughout North Carolina. Simmons knew that Waddell had the connections needed to promote their white supremacy cause. In 1882, Waddell became the editor of the *Charlotte Journal* before returning to Wilmington to practice law. He even canvassed for Grover Cleveland in North Carolina, who would end up winning the presidency. Finally, Waddell was also a member of the Ku Klux Klan Committee and, as such, advocated the statewide white supremacy campaign of 1898 in Wilmington. Waddell united with his political party in support of their white supremacy campaign and used both his gift in oration and his knowledge of the media to the group's advantage.

Waddell joined Simmons speaker's bureau and was seen right away as a symbol of whites who were oppressed under the new world of Reconstruction. Waddell had the uncanny ability to distort the facts to his liking. Instead of portraying the white mobs for what they were – murderous racists – he painted them as heroes. In his mind, they were law-abiding white citizens just doing their duty and restoring law and order. He also portrayed them as executing violence for self-defense; they were not committing crimes, they were defending law and order.

The Democrats presented their largest political rally on October 20, 1898 in Fayetteville, North Carolina. This is where the party's intimidation wing, the Red Shirts, made its debut. This armed gang of white men wore red tunics for uniforms and was used to threaten and intimidate both Populists and Republicans, regardless of race. They broke up anti-Democratic meetings, prevented certain Populist and Republican candidates from speaking, and even beat and whipped African Americans. Ben Tillman, a South Carolina senator who also held white supremacy views, was their party's guest speaker at the event. Senator Tillman was well known for ridiculing blacks on the floor of the United States Senate and even boasted as to help killing them during South Carolina's 1876 gubernatorial campaign. When Senator Tillman had a rally in Fayetteville in October, this would be the first appearance of the paramilitary Red Shirts. At the North Carolina event in 1898, the senator bragged about how he and the Red Shirts used force and deception to take over the power in South Carolina. He urged his North Carolina counterparts to do the same – why weren't they already using violence to get what they want? Why weren't they using violence to silence certain media outlets like Manly? He chastened the crowd of North Carolina racists, questioning why, when it came to Manly and his editorial, "Why didn't you kill that damn nigger editor who wrote that?...Send him to South Carolina and let him publish any such offensive stuff, and he will be killed." In the eyes of the North Carolina Conservative Democrats, Tillman was a white supremacy champion.

Waddell also delivered a speech right in Wilmington on October 24, 1898 that promised to "choke the current of the Cap Fear with carcasses" to again fight what he and his followers called "Negro domination," Along with 50 of Wilmington's most prominent citizens, Waddell orated about white supremacy and how anyone who did not support this single issue should be considered a traitor and held accountable for their actions (or lack thereof). According to Waddell, "the very first men that ought to be held to account are the white leaders of the Negroes who will be chiefly responsible for it. ...I mean the governor of this state who is the engineer of all the deviltry." Waddell was not just chastising blacks; instead, he was also pinning whites who supported blacks – including North Carolina's governor – as an enemy that must be stopped. He was now framing the Fusionists – both the Populists and the Republicans who currently held office – as their adversaries. This move would prove to be beneficial when later they would end up taking over their political offices by force. No one would question this coup d'etat when they already looked at the white men in office as their enemies. Waddell, however, would end up closing his speech by rounding back to the main enemy, which was the blacks: "We will never surrender to a ragged raffle of Negroes".

Yet, Simmons and Waddell were not the only prominent Democrats who led the white supremacy fight. Charles Brantley Aycock practiced law before becoming involved in politics and, in particular, the Democratic cause of white supremacy. He joined Waddell in October 1898 to make speeches that denounced what the two men called a Negro domination. Their speeches worked – Waddell and Aycock took their anti-black, white supremacist speeches across the state and enthused the already felt anti-black sentiments.

Aycock, Waddell, and other prominent white men would continue to rally their base through speeches, printed materials, and even a "White Supremacy Convention" on October 28, 1898 in Goldsboro that reiterated the "Negro domination" phrase perpetuated by Simmons and the conservative media outlets. Waddell, Aycock, Simmons, along with North Carolina Governor Thomas Jarvis and Durham Mayor William A. Guthrie. In front of a crowd of 8,000 white Democrats, the men imparted their white supremacist views and accusations against blacks. After the men used the power of oration to disseminate their racist views, they then used the power of intimidation through their group of Red Shirts.

THE RED SHIRTS

The Democratic leaders knew they needed to scare their opponents into not voting since, at the time, the economy of North Carolina was actually pretty positive. North Carolina saw a massive commercial expansion through the 1890s, and employment opportunities for both whites and blacks had exploded. How would the Democrats fight these positives on Election Day? They would scare, intimidate, and lie their way to the top, all while continuing to spout their rumors about the Fusionists connection to what they continued to call a "Negro domination."

The Red Shirts were an armed gang of white men who terrorized both black citizens and their white supporters – they kidnapped individuals and tortured them, destroyed their homes and property, and ambushed innocent victims who were Republican and Populist supporters. Both Republican and Populist candidates felt the Democratic rage and ended up being too scared of violent attacks to even speak in Wilmington and the surrounding areas. The Red Shirts continuously broke up any meetings that were deemed anti-Democratic to prevent the candidates from speaking to their supporters. By the time the 1898 election came to pass, individuals who would have voted for Republican or Populist tickets were either too afraid to register to vote, or too afraid to vote come Election Day.

Although the Democratic Party spread its white supremacy campaign across North Carolina, Wilmington would become the center for this campaign of racism and violence. Leading up to the election, the Red Shirts patrolled every street in Wilmington to make sure only those who would vote Democrat would actually vote on November 8th. They intimidated and attacked black citizens to the point that, on Election Day, it was a day of terror for those who came in the path of the Red Shirts. Due to the power of the Red Shirts, whites and blacks were both anticipating violence on Election Day. As reported in the *Maxton Blade,* "just before election day [the Red Shirts] made nightly raids, shot through houses, and warned Negroes not to go near the polls." On Election Day, the Red Shirts blocked every road that lead into Maxton, but Maxton was not the only area affected. Communities across North Carolina would be blocked by the Red Shirts, and if blacks did try to break through the blockades to vote, they would be met with gunfire.

Under the guidance of the Democrats' racially-inflammatory campaign, the Red Shirts turned North Carolina's streets into a warzone; they were an organized group of often masked men armed with rifles, shotguns, and pistols. They used their intimidation tactics to prevent non-Democrats from getting to the polls to vote, and they even terrorized then Republican Governor Daniel L. Russell Jr. Russell had observed the tactics of the Red Shirts and complained on the days leading up to Election Day about the intimidation and terror tactics. He even withdrew the Republican ticket from New Hanover County to try to stop the violence. This olive branch would prove futile, however. Governor Russell was able to vote in his hometown of Wilmington on November 8th, but when he was returning by train to Raleigh he would come face-to-face with the infamous Red Shirts. The Red Shirts stopped his train twice, and the governor would end up hiding in a railroad mail car in Hamlet, North Carolina after he voted in order to evade the Red Shirts who were after him.

NOVEMBER 8, 1898 –
ELECTION DAY

With North Carolina's Election Day approaching, wealthy Democrats used the power of their money to help the Democrats and their issue of white supremacy. These prominent white men gave free food and alcohol to white mobs, donated money for weapons, and even hosted a "White Man's Rally" on November 2nd to celebrate white supremacy via a barbeque and parade. All of these events leading up to the election illustrated the strength the Democrats had built and how this strength would affect Election Day.

The night before the election, Waddell reiterated this strength and the violence that was expected: "You are Anglo-Saxons. You are armed and prepared, and you will do your duty. If you find the Negro out voting, tell him to leave the polls, and if he refuses, kill him, shoot him down in his tracks. We shall win tomorrow if we have to do it with guns." Waddell's words did not go unnoticed - on November 8, 1898, Wilmington's Democratic Party and their masses of white supporters took matters into their own hands to overturn the Republican-Populist control.

Under their leader, Waddell, the whites in Wilmington mobilized, held white supremacist rallies and parades, and begun unleashing their militarized band of Red Shirts to intimidate blacks from voting, Republicans from canvassing, and disseminate threatening calls to anyone and everyone against them. Many blacks would stay home on Election Day for fear of their lives, and the ones who did try to vote were met with armed white men. The Democrats had developed a successful campaign of violence and

36

intimidation, yet they were still compelled to cheat. The Democrats stuffed ballot boxes with their own candidates and threw out the Republican ballots, just in case their violent barrages were not enough to take over the elections. The Democrats were successful in first suppressing the Republican and Populist votes, and then committing voter fraud to successfully steal the election.

The racist Democratic propaganda, intimidation, violence, and fraud were all successful tools to breed hate and take over North Carolina politics – they won the Wilmington elections by 6,000 votes. Then, the Democrats used an August 18, 1898 editorial written by Alexander Manley, the African-American owner of the newspaper, the *Wilmington Daily Record*. Manley had used his editorial status to respond to the lynching of blacks who were deemed by racist whites as "rapists." In particular, he was responding to accusations made by Rebecca Felton in a speech in 1897 in Georgia that would end up being reprinted in the *Wilmington Messenger*.

Alexander Manly was a highly educated man of mixed-race descent. His father, Charles Manly, had actually been the governor of North Carolina from 1849 through 1851. This fact made Manly that much more credible when he started questioning things in his newspaper on that fateful day. Manly himself was the product of a white man possibly intimidating a black woman into sex, and the result was a child of mixed race. Yet, Manly may have never responded to the racial outbreak in Wilmington if it had not been for an editorial in the *Wilmington Messenger* written by Georgia native Rebecca Felton. Felton was already well-known in conservative circles; her husband, William H. Felton, won the Seventh Congressional District seat in Georgia in 1874 as an Independent Democrat and this urged Rebecca to enter the political arena as well. She wrote both her husband's speeches and numerous newspaper articles on his behalf. But it would be a speech that she did under her own name, which was reprinted in the *Wilmington Messenger,* that would spark controversy. Although she was a staunch lynching supporter, Rebecca Felton would end up being the first woman to serve in the United States Senate when she was honored with an appointment, although she only served for one day.

On August 11, 1897, Rebecca Felton presented a speech to the Georgia Agricultural Society. Among other things, Felton made claims that farm wives faced the ultimate danger of black rapists. During this speech, she claimed that, "When there is not enough religion in the pulpit to organize a crusade against sin; nor justice in the courthouse to promptly punish crime; nor manhood enough in the nation to put a sheltering arm about innocence and virtue." And she implored that, "if it needs lynching to protect woman's dearest possession form the ravening human beasts----then I say lynch, a thousand times a week if necessary," Felton was urging the white Southern men to lynch blacks, and when this speech was reprinted in the *Wilmington Messenger,* Manly was compelled to respond in his own newspaper.

In response to the reprint of Felton's original speech, Manly tried to illustrate that the fear-mongering of rape and call for mass murder of black men was fictitious. Manly opined that not all interracial sexual encounters are a result of rape. In fact, he pointed out how sexual contact between black men and white women could actually be consensual, not coerced. He also pointed out a disturbing fact that many white men regularly seduced and even raped black women, yet this would not be discussed during Felton's outcries. He questioned why it was evil for a black man to intimidate a white woman, yet it was not evil for a white man to intimidate a black woman.

More specifically, Manly wrote that "poor white men are careless in the matter of protecting their women." He paraphrased African-American journalist Ida B. Wells, who also investigated lynchings, advocated for the arming of black citizens, and was a civil rights leader in her own right, while also lecturing to his readers about how "our experience among poor white people in the country teaches us that women of that race are not any more particular in the matter of clandestine meetings with colored men than the white men with the colored women." Wells would end up being a prominent activist later when Jim Crow laws were in full force after she refused to leave a first-class train car that was designated as "whites only." She was forcefully removed by the conductor and she successfully sued the railroad (a decision that was later reversed, however, in higher court). Wells was the perfect activist to be quoted by Manly. In fact, in 1889, she became the co-owner of the Memphis *Free Speech and Headlight,* a publication she used to promote her positions on early Jim Crows laws like school segregation and sexual harassment of blacks. But a mob would end up destroying her newspaper and Wells ended up moving to the North after her life was threatened.

Now, in the 1800s, it was already well-known that the subject of interracial sex was deemed offensive and distasteful. Yet, Manley magnified this issue in his opinion piece, arguing that, in many cases, the accusations of rape after a black man had sex with a white woman were not fact but, instead, the result of the white woman willingly having an affair with a black man. This editorial did not just anger and rile up the Democrats; the leaders in the Democratic Party saw the piece as the gift they needed to further their propaganda about predatory black men.

Both Simmons and Waddell used Manly's editorials as a gift. Simmons raged about Manly's actions, calling it an assailment on the virtue of their white women, while privately celebrating Manly's words and how they could be used to their advantage. Waddell also used Manley's "gift" to his advantage in his speeches to continue to spread his group's message of racism, hate, and violence. He essentially used it as a catalyst for the violence, and between Waddell's hateful prose and the Red Shirts violently intimidating black voters and disrupting Republican meetings, the Democrats won unquestionable victories when North Carolina citizens voted on November 8, 1898. The election was stolen through the use of violence, but that would not be enough for the conservatives. They would continue their reign of racism through two final acts. First, the white Democrats decided to perform what is called a coup d'etat – the forcible removal, using violence, of an existing government. Then, nearly 2,000 white conservative men took to violence again and burned down the building that housed Manly's newspaper, the *Wilmington Daily Record*.

AMERICA'S ONLY COUP D'ETAT

The Democrats successfully stole an election, but that would not be enough for the conservatives. Even after the election was over, Wilmington was still viewed as a symbol of African-American political and economic power. White Democrats were ready to change that immediately. While the violence set off by their band of Red Shirts was raging, white leaders unleashed their very own coup d'etat.

Although the Democrats were able to steal most of the political seats through violent intimidation and force, they were not able to take them all. For one, not all local Wilmington seats were up for re-election on November 8, 1898. Wilmington in particular had many Fusionist government officials still in office – Mayor Silas, the board of aldermen, and the police chief. So, they took matters into their own hands. First, one of the "Secret Nine," Hugh MacRae, called for a public meeting in the *Wilmington Messenger*. This meeting consisted of prominent white businessmen who all had the same goal – run the Fusionists and the blacks out of town.

The group of men called for the resignations of the Republican Mayor Silas P. Wright, the board of alderman, and even Police Chief John Melton, but would end up forcing them to resign (while holding them at gunpoint). Mayor Wright had been a target of the Democrats from the beginning due to two things: he was a Northerner, originally from Massachusetts, making him a carpetbagger (a political candidate that runs for election in an area in which he or she does not have local connections). What was probably more offensive to the Democrats, however, was that Mayor Wright had helped put black men in office.

The white supremacists who followed Waddell, Simmons, ridiculed Mayor Wright, making it easy to accept his forced resignation. Waddell and his faithful followers formalized their political control on Wilmington with Waddell as mayor who was surrounded by all Democratic aldermen. By 4 p.m., the new mayor of Wilmington was Col. Alfred M. Waddell and the city was run by wealthy conservatives.

A Committee of Colored Citizens was called to hear the whites' demands on November 9th. More than twenty whites and thirty prominent African Americans were called to the courthouse, where Waddell read to them what they called the White Declaration of Independence. The document began by noting how the United States Constitution had anticipated that the government was to be run by enlightened people, which did not include those of African origin, before then declaring that:

"We, the undersigned citizens of the City of Wilmington and County of New Hanover, do hereby declare that we will no longer be ruled, and will never again be ruled by men of African origin. This condition we have in part endured because we felt that the consequences of the War of Secession were such as to deprive us of the fair consideration of many of our countrymen. We believe that, after more than thirty years, this is no longer the case".

This was the exact document that, on August 6, 2017, the North Carolina GOP Executive Director, Dallas Woodhouse, referenced in his tweets. The document concluded with seven expectations of their all-white city, demanding specifically that Manly leave the city forever within twenty-four hours of Waddell's proclamation. Not only did Manly leave (he had actually already fled the city before this proclamation), but more than 2,000 blacks permanently left Wilmington, turning what was once a black-majority into a white-majority Wilmington. By 4 p.m. on November 11, 1868, former Confederate officer turned white supremacy leader, Alfred Moore Waddell, would be crowned the mayor of Wilmington. And, the new mayor already had powerful backings, as H. Leon Prather noted: "the Secret Nine furnished him with a list of prominent Republicans, both white and black, who must be banished from Wilmington."

The Committee of Colored Citizens drafted a response, although at this point their response would not matter or stop the violence: "We the colored citizens to whom was referred the matter of expulsion from this community of the person and press of A.L. Manly beg most respectfully to say that we are in no wise responsible for nor in anyway condone the obnoxious article that called forth your actions. Neither are we authorized to act for him in this matter; but in the interest of peace, we will most willingly use our influence to have your wishes carried out."

The group had one of their youngest most fit members hand deliver their written response to Waddell. The young man, however, was blocked by armed whites and, after hearing gunshots, decided against hand delivering the message and instead made way to the post office. Waddell would end up scheduling a meeting at the Light Infantry Armory, awaiting a response from the Committee of Colored Citizens. But the letter was never delivered, which infuriated Waddell. What did he then do? He led his men to Manly's press building that housed the *Wilmington Daily Record.*

THE RIOT OF WILMINGTON

Through a new White Declaration of Independence, Waddell quickly ordered Manly to leave Wilmington by the morning of November 10th; Manly had already left, escaping the violence that would befall upon his newspaper when a mob of hundreds upon hundreds of white men would smash through and burn down his building. Yet, Manly and other African Americans living in Wilmington could have never known that, on that chilly November 10th day, a group of heavily armed white men would march into the black neighborhoods, under the guise of white supremacy, and take over the political landscape of what was once the perfect representation of African-American economic and political success.

In 1898, Wilmington was a prosperous port town that sat on where the Cape Fear River entered into the Atlantic Ocean. Yet, on November 10, 1868, Waddell caroused a group of nearly 2,000 angry and heavily armed white men to the Love and Charity Hall building, where the newspaper the *Wilmington Daily Record* was published. Seven blocks east of the Cape Fear River, the angry, racist mob, led by Waddell, pummeled through the door, doused the building with kerosene, and set it on fire. By nightfall, Manly's newspaper had been torched beyond belief – the building that housed the *Wilmington Daily Record* was burned to the ground. To make matters worse, some of the whites involved in the arson actually posed for a photograph in front of the building, guns held in front of them, to honor and memorialize the destruction. This was just the beginning, however, of the white supremacist violence.

The symbol of the burning building enraged blacks, and soon the streets were full of fuming blacks and whites. But, the Democrats were ready – their band of violent Red Shirts rode in on horseback to further terrorize the black community and their white supporters. Some more prominent blacks were specific targets; for example, the black politician Daniel Wright was pulled from his home, beaten, and almost killed before the gang of violent whites encouraged him to run. The white mob, however, would not show him any mercy and, instead, shot him so many times his body was literally ripped to pieces. Thomas Clawson, editor of the *Wilmington Messenger,* documented the violence as "a volley tore off the top of a [black]man's head and he fell dead about 20 feet in front of the newshawks."

By the time the violence in Wilmington subsided, it was estimated that hundreds had died. Not only that, but the white mob collected in front of Wilmington's city jail while soldiers marched Fusionist leaders to the train station – 21 blacks, along with their white allies, would be exiled from the city of Wilmington on that fateful day. African-American leaders and businessmen, such as business leaders Salem J. Bell and Robert B. Pickens, and white politicians who did not hold Conservative Democratic values – they were all the same in the minds of the white mob. In fact, a white Fusionist and deputy sheriff George Z. French barely escaped being lynched himself when a white mob placed a noose around his neck and started to hang him from a street light. If it was not for a member of the Committee of Twenty-Five, Frank Stedman, who saved French's life, he would have been killed alongside his black counterparts. French was not completely saved; instead, the angry mob dragged him to the train station and forced him to leave North Carolina. The chief of police, John Melton, was also confronted by the mob and, if not for the soldiers that stopped the mob, would have also been lynched. Melton was a steadfast Populist, which automatically made him the enemy to his white conservative counterparts.

Many other African Americans were said to have escaped to the swamps or even hid in African-American cemeteries with the hopes of not getting caught by the angry, racist white mob that had befallen upon Wilmington. Four days after the coup d'etat, hundreds of African Americans who escaped the wrath of the white mobs hid in the forests around their city of Wilmington. Many had escaped so quickly that they left all of their belongings and did not even have a coat or blanket for warmth. Mothers, fathers, and their children shivered in the cold, knowing it was better than the murder that was happening in their once-home city of black hope. Charles Francis Bourke of *Collier's Weekly* documented what he heard as "a child crying and a hoarse voice crooning softly a mournful song, the words of which fell into my memory with the air: 'When de battle over we kin wear a crown in the new Je-ru-sulum.'"

On November 11, 1898, one day after the violent takeover by the Conservative Democrats, a military parade marched down the streets of Wilmington. The statewide Democratic Party threw a party in Raleigh and, as the days continued, the whites who agreed with the Democrats would dismiss the mass murder as needed to overthrow and instill their own form of government. Not only were the events that happened that fateful day in Wilmington, North Carolina some of the most gruesome attacks on blacks and allied whites in history. It was also the only coup d'etat to ever take place on American soil. By the end of the day, Manly's newspaper was incinerated, an insurmountable amount of people were murdered in cold blood, and the local government was overthrown and replaced with white supremacists. What is even worse? It would take more than 100 years for the true story of the Wilmington Insurrection of 1898 to be told, as it was lost in history for more than a century. The murders were viewed as heroes and the blacks as riotous villains. Blacks were erroneously described as instigators while the racist whites were looked at as saviors.

THE RISE OF WHITE SUPREMACY

Finally, after more than 100 years, it is documented that a mob of armed white supremacists marched through Wilmington, North Carolina, overthrew a legitimately elected government, forced both black and white officials to resign and leave town, and torch a black newspaper's building to the ground. Then what happened? All the black and Fusionist city employees were fired and school committees were declared to be all white (even in primarily black districts). A number of black residents in Wilmington were killed, with the help of the Red Shirts, and even the governor could not help his citizens. Governor Russell tried to direct the state militia to stop the violence, but still blacks were only arrested by the Democratic commander, Walker Taylor.

November 10, 1898 would end up being the day white supremacists murdered African Americans in the primarily black city of Wilmington, North Carolina, overthrew the elected Reconstruction-era based government, elected only two days earlier, in a coup d'etat, and birthed decades of racist laws against blacks. Wilmington, which was once a haven for black and white integration in the South, shifted into a city dominated by white supremacy in just a matter of days. However, this is not just a story of a burned building, lynchings, and violence – it is a story of the lives of black citizens that were lost along with the spirit of their black community.

President William McKinley did receive letters from concerned citizens pleading for help during and after Wilmington's violence, but in the end, no one could help the black community. The true story of the violence and hate were nearly lost forever, yet these events were the basis of post-slavery racial politics and, later, "Jim Crow." The coup was deemed a success for the white supremacists and their staunch followers of the white, prominent business elite. Along with brothers Alex and Frank Manly, who were forced to leave after their newspaper was burned to the ground, it has been estimated that more than 2,000 blacks permanently left Wilmington, North Carolina. Waddell ended up being mayor for the next seven years. He died in 1912.

The effects of the Wilmington Insurrection of 1898 did not stop after that racist, violent day. The following year, the new Conservative legislature enacted its first order of business: disenfranchise blacks. In 1900, Democrats won the governor's office using many similar campaign tactics they used in 1898. That same year, Democrats passed the Suffrage Amendment to the North Carolina State Constitution, which eliminated African-American voting rights and maintained segregation that would last until Civil Rights movements in the 1950s and 1960s. Not only that, but the North Carolina suffrage amendment also held a grandfather clause that stated that an illiterate person could not vote unless their father or grandfather voted prior to 1867 (which eliminated many blacks from voting). In order to vote they must pass a literacy test. These are just some of the many white supremacy effects felt in North Carolina and across the United States, and they all stemmed from Wilmington. In a sense, the effects of the Wilmington Insurrection of 1898 would be felt for more than 60 years.

This was only the beginning; in the years that followed, the leaders of this white supremacy campaign would be fundamentally responsible for what would be known as "Jim Crow laws." Democrats were set on developing racial hierarchy laws that would prohibit blacks and whites from doing the most basic things together in everyday life. This was the world of Jim Crow – whether it was sitting together on a bus or train, getting an education, even reading the Bible, whites and blacks would be required by law to do these acts separately. Jim Crow was essentially a collection of both state and local statutes that legalized racial segregation. Among other things, they would remove the freedoms blacks had to hold certain jobs, get an education, frequent service industries, even to vote. These laws would remain on the legal books until 1968, and they all started because of the events in Wilmington.

North Carolina Democrats specifically began passing a flood of Jim Crow laws in 1899. But, these laws were not just in North Carolina, but on a massive scale across the country. Although the Wilmington Insurrection of 1898 may not have invented these laws, they certainly did strengthen and bolster them over time. It is understandable that the roots of Jim Crow could be seen immediately following the ratification of the Thirteenth Amendment in 1865 in which slavery in the United States was officially abolished. The Ku Klux Klan was also born that year in Pulaski, Tennessee and would be the main group that terrorized blacks over time. But, it was after the 1898 violence that, through Jim Crow, white supremacy was infused into nearly every aspect of daily life.

Jim Crow laws forbid African Americans from entering everything from restaurants and theatres to restrooms and train stations. They even segregated water fountains to black and white only. African Americans could not live in white areas, they could not attend white schools, and their children could not play in white parks. Some states even forced that white and black children learn from separate textbooks. And, marriage and cohabitation between whites and black was forbidden in most of the Southern states.

The Wilmington Insurrection of 1898 led to white supremacy, Jim Crow, and, eventually, more race riots. In the 20th century, lynching had become so prevalent in the Southern states that, in 1919 alone, 25 race riots transpired across the United States. Prior to 1898, blacks and whites lived together in Wilmington. Yet, within one year, physical segregation increased under Jim Crow. Home values, social statuses, and the overall quality of life would be quite different between the races in Wilmington. And, North Carolina would end up being an example to other Southern states. Through 1908, many other Southern states followed North Carolina's lead and also suppressed the black vote through disenfranchisement Jim Crow laws or constitutional amendments. They also followed the lead of North Carolina by passing laws that mandated racial segregation in public facilities and everyday life. Jim Crow was everywhere.

Jim Crow laws would not even be tested until 1948, when President Harry Truman ordered integration in the United States military. Then in 1954, the United States Supreme Court ruled on the now infamous *Brown versus the Board of Education*, which made educational segregation unconstitutional. President Lyndon B. Johnson continued the war on Jim Crow in 1964 when he signed the Civil Rights Act, which legally ended the segregation that was established by Jim Crow laws. Race riots, however, would continue throughout the mid- to late-1960s. There were some very well-known riots, such as the 1967 Detroit riot, and some lesser known riots in smaller cities and towns. From 1964 through 1971, more than 750 riots hit cities across the country, resulting in more than 200 deaths and nearly 13,000 injuries. The year 1967 alone had nearly 200 disorders reported, and then racial conflicts and violence exploded again a year later after Dr. Martin Luther King Jr.'s assassination on April 4, 1968. This upsurge of racial violence affected more than one hundred cities across the United States.

Although race riots have toned down in recent years, white supremacy has not. According to Neil MacFarquhar and Adam Goldman (January 22, 2020) of the *New York Times,* there is an increase in racially motived violent extremism in the United States. "The details that emerged in court and in documents from active cases in three other states — Georgia, Wisconsin and New Jersey — unveiled a disturbing new face of white supremacy." White supremacy may have been compelled by the events in 1898, but new cases illustrate that it still holds true today.

The state of North Carolina would also go through more tumultuous times when it came to racial disparities and white supremacy. Even after President Johnson signed the Voting Rights Act in 1965, which was a landmark piece of legislation in the world of racial discrimination, North Carolina voters still fought struggles at the ballot. The literacy tests discussed earlier remained in place until 1975, yet by 1980 the number of registered black voters still did not rise in relation to other states.

For more than a century, the story of the Wilmington Insurrection of 1898 was not truthfully told. In fact, a biography capsule of one of the Insurrection masterminds – Alfred Moore Waddell – encapsulates exactly what students who learned about this time were taught. They were not taught about the racist views of the Conservative Democrats, the murders at the hands of the Red Shirts, the forced takeover of a legally-elected government. Instead:

"The Democrats and most white citizens of the State feared a return to the corrupt and financially devastating rule of Republicans as had been experienced during reconstruction in the late 1860's. Waddell led white Wilmingtonians in their effort to shut down a racially-inflammatory black newspaper, and then became mayor of Wilmington after the unpopular Republican regime had resigned. As mayor, 'Waddell quickly restored sobriety and peace, demonstrating his capacity to act with courage in critical times.' He continued in this office until 1905, leading a responsible and honest government unaffected by the racial turbulence of his predecessor."

After knowing the truth of what happened in the days leading up to the Wilmington Insurrection of 1898 – the calculated plan by the Conservative Democrats – the information quoted by Waddell above is disconcerting to say the least. Yet, this is the story that was told to students – not a story of murderous whites but, instead, a story of whites fighting an unpopular Republican regime and racial turbulence. In the words of Waddell, the Democrats and their white followers were simply fighting the corrupt Republicans. Manly's newspaper was racially inflammatory and Waddell was a savior. Obviously these were lies, but the lies would be told for more than 100 years. Even in the 1990s, Waddell was still portrayed as a virtuous campaigner, someone who fought for the peace of Wilmington. According to historian David S. Cecelski, "I had a book in my middle-school classroom that listed the 12 greatest North Carolinians ever. It included the Wright brothers, Virginia Dare, and then it included three of the people who were the leaders of the white supremacy campaign." For more than a century, the perpetrators of the racially-violent acts that destroyed lives were cast as heroes in student's history books. And what is even worse, the blacks who were the victims were painted as the original instigators of the violence.

It was not until 2006 that the events in Wilmington that remained hidden from history for so many years would come to light. It would be then – 108 years later – that North Carolina would finally complete its full investigation of the racial violence that had befallen on Wilmington. Historians pieced this together this story by reading newspaper articles from across North Carolina to get a sense of the time frame. The violence was everywhere – black newspapers were burned down across North Carolina, not just Wilmington. The story of the Wilmington Insurrection of 1898 started to fall into place. And this time, it was the true story.

It would be then that a Wilmington Race Riot Commission would conclude that the tragedy "marked a new epoch in the history of violent race relations in the United States." In fact, the Commission would even recommend payments to the descendants of the victims and warn media outlets, including the infamous *News and Observer,* to retell the story – the truth – about what actually happened in November of 1898. November 10th was not a spontaneous race riot caused by blacks; instead, it was a calculated campaign thought up by a group of racist, white Democrats: steal elections, start a riot, stage a coup d'etat, and finally, banish the opposition.

Many individuals found it shocking that in 2017 – 119 years after the racial violence in Wilmington – GOP Executive Director, Dallas Woodhouse, would bring up this stain in North Carolina's history. But, one good thing came out of his tweets – remembrance of what really happened on November 10, 1898 in Wilmington, North Carolina.

Made in United States
North Haven, CT
25 April 2025

68297541R00036

THE
WILMINGTON
INSURRECTION OF 1898

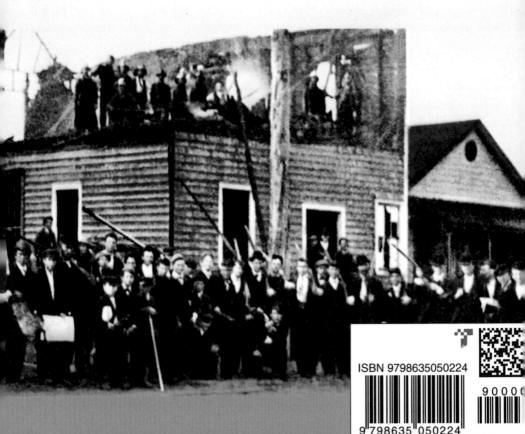

ISBN 9798635050224

Louis Charbonneau=Lassay

THE
BESTIARY
OF
CHRIST

Translated & Abridged by D.M. Dooling